I0163746

Joseph

James Poole

ISBN: 978-1-78364-459-9

The Open Bible Trust
Fordland Mount, Upper Basildon,
Reading, RG8 8LU, UK.

www.obt.org.uk

Unless indicated otherwise Scripture quotations are taken from the New King James Version®. Copyright © 1982 by Thomas Nelson. Used by permission. All rights reserved.

Joseph

Contents

Page

Introduction

"*All* Scripture is given by inspiration of God and is profitable for doctrine, for reproof, for correction, for instruction in righteousness that the man of God may be complete, throughly equipped for every good work." (2 Timothy 3:16-17; RAV)

So then, let us turn to the Old Testament and study the life of one of its outstanding characters, Joseph. In my opinion, of all the four patriarchs, Joseph stands out head and shoulders above the other three, Abraham, Isaac and Jacob.

The record of his life is given to us in the book of Genesis, chapters 37-50, and before continuing with this publication you may care to read those pages of the Old Testament.

James Poole

Joseph

Joseph was truly a chosen vessel of the Lord. His consistent faith in God never dimmed, neither do we hear any murmur or complaint from him while undergoing adversity in prison, nor did his exaltation to be virtually Prime Minister of Egypt turn his head. In this respect Joseph is truly a magnificent type of Christ Himself, in his suffering and the glory that followed him.

We must bear in mind that we are most privileged to live in an era different from the one Joseph lived in. We live in an era that is a Day of Grace. God is at present reconciled to the whole world of sinners, beseeching them to receive His peace and salvation through the precious blood of Christ. It is for us, as individuals, to lay aside our enmity to God and respond to His gracious offer, which is in and through our Lord Jesus Christ! "Behold now is the accepted time: behold now is the day of salvation!" (2 Corinthians 6:2).

Nevertheless, in all the great characters which we find in the Old Testament, there are certain principles of faith and obedience that are for our guidance and instruction, if we "rightly divide the Word of Truth" (2 Timothy 2:15).

Joseph the boy

Joseph was born of Rachel, Jacob's wife, the one he loved above all his other wives and concubines. No wonder Jacob adored Joseph his son by Rachel. The early life of Joseph is not told to us. He was born beyond the Euphrates river, in what was called Mesopotamia and is now called Iraq, some 400 miles from the Promised Land (Genesis 30:22-24). His early years were spent in Paddan Aram, where his father was serving Laban, Jacob's uncle (Genesis 46:15; 28:2).

Joseph the teenage

So much for Joseph's earlier life. We begin with him, a lad of seventeen years old, and find him feeding his father Jacob's flock, with his brothers, Dan and Naphtali, the sons of Bilhah, Rachael's maid servant, and Gad and Asher, the sons of Leah's maid servant Zilpah.

It is evident that the brothers were misbehaving themselves and neglecting their duty to the flock, for Joseph told his father of their evil deeds (Genesis 37:2).

As schoolboys, we would probably say that Joseph was a sneak! This is by no means true. Dan, Naphtali, Gad and Asher were the sons of slave girls and, as such, had no statutory rights. Moreover in Genesis 35:22 and 1 Chronicles 5:1-2 we are told that Reuben, Jacob's firstborn son, committed a shameful act of incest with Bilhah, his father's concubine, and Israel (Jacob) heard of it and took away the rights and privileges of a firstborn son and gave them to Joseph.

We must remember that a Hebrew firstborn son was given by his father a certain jurisdiction over his brothers, which he could exercise in his father's absence.

Joseph was the apple of his father's eye and Jacob gave him a distinctive garment (a coat of many colours KJV), which was a symbol of rank, as heir of all the authority and privileges of a firstborn son. No doubt Joseph's brothers resented him for acting as an overseer for their father Jacob. Thus they came to hate him.

Joseph's dreams

Now Joseph had two dreams which he told to his brothers and his father. The first dream portrayed them binding sheaves of corn in the field. Joseph's sheaf stood upright, but his brothers' sheaves made obeisance to his sheaf. This was a future prediction of Joseph being sent to Egypt to preserve life there during a great famine, and his family would be dependent on him for sustenance.

In the second dream the sun, moon and stars made obeisance to Joseph, which portrayed him as a highly exalted prince and ruler among his family.

These two dreams were not just youthful fancies but God given visions of what lay ahead for Joseph in the future. He told the second dream to his father and brothers. His brothers hated him yet more, but his father, after rebuking him, took note of it (Genesis 37:5-11).

Joseph and Jesus

Let us pause for a moment and consider the great antitype of Joseph, our Lord Jesus Christ. Like Jacob, God the Father reveals His great love for His Son. "This is my beloved Son in Whom I am well pleased" (Matthew 3:17). Like Joseph, who was given authority over his brothers, God gave all things into His Son's hands; "The Father loves the Son, and has given all things into his hand" (John 3:35).

Like Joseph also, our Lord was hated by His brethren, the nation of Israel. His words and blameless life exposed their evil ways. "We will not have this man to reign over us" (Luke 19:14), was an echo of the words of Joseph's brothers; "And his brothers said to him, 'Shall you indeed reign over us? Or shall you indeed have dominion over us?' So they hated him even more for his dreams and for his words" (Genesis 37:8).

Joseph and his brothers

Now Joseph's brothers went to feed their father's flock in Shechem. It was there that Dinah, Jacob's daughter by his wife Leah, was disgraced. Shechem, the son of Hamor the Hivite, fell in love with Dinah and wanted to marry her after intimacy with her. This would mean marriage with an uncircumcised alien, which was forbidden to the tribe of Israel. But two of Jacob's sons, Simeon and Levi, took a cruel and ruthless revenge. They slew Hamor and Shechem his son and took all their livestock, wealth, wives and children captive. This caused Jacob's name to stink among the Hivites (Genesis 34:25-30).

I have brought in this incident to show why Jacob sent Joseph to Shechem to find out how things were with Joseph's brothers. Jacob may have anticipated some retaliatory action on the part of the men of Shechem, the Hivites, in return for what they had suffered at the hands of Simeon and Levi.

So Joseph sets out but finds that his brothers had departed from Shechem and gone to Dothan, which was on the high road to Egypt for trader's caravans from the East. There he found them, but they had seen him coming from afar off and they conspired against Joseph to slay him. But God was with Joseph. Instead of permitting his brother to kill him, He allowed the calmer counsel of Reuben and Judah to prevail. Joseph was cast into a pit and sold to a passing company of Midianites, on their way to trade in Egypt.

Joseph and Jesus

So Joseph became a slave in Egypt to Potiphar, Captain of the Guard, a kind of Chief of Police with military duties also (Genesis 37:21-28, 36). Joseph's abduction by his brothers, their casting him into a pit intending to slay him, portrayed our Lord's betrayal and crucifixion. Joseph's brothers conspired against him to slay him. So did the Chief Priest and rulers of the nation of Israel conspire against the Lord Jesus (Matthew 27:1).

The callous indifference of Joseph's brothers to his fate (Genesis 37:25), was similar to that of the soldiers, who nailed our Lord to the cross (Matthew 27:36).

Judah sold Joseph for 20 Shekels of silver. Judas sold Christ for 30 pieces of silver (Matthew 26:15).

Jacob, Joseph's father, keenly felt the loss of his son who was greatly beloved by him. History often repeats incidents in life which are similar.

Jacob deceived his father Isaac with the skin of a kid, when he stole the birthright which belonged to Esau, his brother (Genesis 27:21-23). He, in turn, was deceived by the blood of a kid, when his sons brought him Joseph's garment stained with blood which he thought to be that of his favourite son (Genesis 37:31-33).

Joseph and faith

So Joseph finds himself a slave in a strange land, far from home and his beloved father. Did he mope, murmur or complain to the Lord? No! He remembered the dreams he had received – the bowing sheaves and the obeisance of the sun, moon and stars to him. These were God given visions of Joseph's future.

"Faith comes by hearing and hearing by the Word of God" wrote Paul in Romans 10:17. Joseph hung on to these visions by faith, trusting the Lord to fulfil them in due course.

Do we look forward to God's promises to us? Do we set our affections on things above, where Christ is seated at the right hand of God? Do we look forward to that Day when Christ will be manifest in glory, and we with him? (Colossians 3:1-4). If we do it will make a lot of difference to our outlook on life, and is the greatest incentive to a worthy walk.

Joseph and Potiphar

"The Lord was with Joseph" (Genesis 39:2-6).

Even in his adversity did Joseph prosper for Potiphar made him steward over his household. We all know the incident of Potiphar's wife, when she attempted to make Joseph commit adultery. I suggest, and it is only a suggestion, that the temptation was more subtle than the mere gratification of the flesh.

Joseph was on his own and, in spite of his position of authority in Potiphar's household, he was still virtually a slave. If he entered into a clandestine relationship with his master's wife, could she not use her influence to promote him to a more exalted station? Would not this be a short cut to the realisation of his dreams of future glory?

Did not Satan approach our Lord in the wilderness with the temptation to take an easy way to conquer the world? After Satan had shown Christ all the kingdoms of the world, with all their glory, he said:

> "All these things will I give you, if you will fall down and worship me" (Matthew 4:9).

Make no mistake; this was no idle promise of Satan. He had the power to do this, as he will do in the future to the Man of Sin, the Anti-Christ, Satan's Christ. As the god of this world Satan was offering the throne of glory to Christ, but without the way of the cross.

Joseph's experience was like our Lord's, but, like Him, he turned a deaf ear to Potiphar's wife who sought to make him disloyal to God.

To the repeated solicitations of the fair temptress, his answer was …

> "How then can I do this great wickedness and sin against God?" (Genesis 39:7-10).

Joseph's faithfulness to God led him into deeper adversity. A woman scorned is a dangerous adversary! Her lies and false accusations against Joseph to her husband, we are familiar with. Joseph might have been executed but for the hand of God restraining Potiphar, who, in view of Joseph's efficiency as steward, was disposed to be more lenient. Thus Joseph was cast into prison. From the human standpoint, such an unjust punishment for his loyalty to God might have made Joseph despair and complain about his fate.

Joseph in prison

Do we complain when we suffer for righteousness sake? Do we say how unfair it all is? Not so Joseph! His faith in God was as steady as a rock. His expectation in the fulfilment of God's promises was undimmed. He set to work to make himself useful in prison life and under the Lord's hand he prospered.

> "The Lord gave him favour in the sight of the keeper of the prison, who committed to Joseph's hand all the prisoners that were in the prison,"

leaving him completely in charge of them (Genesis 39:21-33).

We are reminded that@

> "God works *all* things together for good to them that love God; to those who are called, according to His purpose" (Romans 8:28).

There is also:

> "the peace of God which passes all understanding" (Philippians 4:7).

It is superior to every frame of mind – the peace Christ gives His own!

That Joseph, in the depth of his adversity, was able to make himself useful in the service of the prison governor was a living witness to the fact that Joseph had that peace of mind.

> "Thou wilt keep him in perfect peace, whose mind is stayed on Thee, because he trusteth in Thee" (Isaiah 26:3).

But God had not only given Joseph peace of mind. He had given him also wisdom in the interpretation of dreams. He was first able to exercise this gift in prison, in the case of his fellow prisoners – Pharaoh's chief cup bearer and chief baker (Genesis 40:5-8).

Joseph and dreams

We all know the story of those dreams and their sequel well, so I will not go into them in detail. The chief cup bearer was restored to Pharaoh's service, but the chief baker was executed (Genesis 40:9-23).

Two years later, Pharaoh himself had a twofold dream; the seven well favoured cows and the seven lean cows. This was followed by a second dream; seven good ears of corn followed by seven thin ears of corn (Genesis 41:1-7).

It was then that the forgetful chief cup bearer remembered Joseph who had successfully interpreted his dream. So Joseph is summoned before Pharaoh and is enabled by his God given wisdom to interpret Pharaoh's dreams – a twofold warning of seven years of plenty to be followed by seven years of famine in the land.

Pharaoh is so impressed with Joseph's wisdom that he exalts him to be virtually Prime Minister of

Egypt. He was also made responsible for the storage and distribution of food in Egypt, in view of the impending famine. Thus according to Joseph's dream of the bowing sheaves, he was sent into Egypt to preserve life.

Joseph and Jesus

Pharaoh gave Joseph a new name, Zaph'enath-paneah – which may mean:

"the abundance of life."

Its true meaning is uncertain and other suggestions are "revealer of secrets", "the god speaks and he lives", and "saviour of the age".

Joseph was 30 years old when he stood before Pharaoh (Genesis 41:46). Luke gives the age of our Lord at the beginning of His ministry as "about 30 years old" (Luke 3:23). One of His titles given by John is "The Bread of Life" (John 6:48).

So just as Joseph began his ministry of supplying the natural bread of life to those who hungered, so Jesus began His ministry of supplying the true Spiritual Bread of Life to hungry souls.

The record that Joseph went about in his chariot as the cry went up before him, "Bow the knee,"

(Genesis 41:43) reminds us of our Lord's exaltation to the right hand of God the Father.

"Therefore God also has highly exalted Him and given Him a Name, which is above every name, that in the Name of Jesus, every knee should bow, of those in heaven and those on earth and of those under the earth, and that every tongue should confess that Jesus Christ is Lord to the glory of God the Father" (Philippians 2:9-11).

Joseph and his brothers

We have seen how Joseph's brothers treated him! We are now going to see how the exalted and triumphant Joseph treats his brothers. They had to be brought to acknowledge their guilt and repent of their evil deed. This was accomplished by Joseph with great wisdom and tenderness, coupled with discipline.

Joseph's brothers resented him spying on them and then reporting their evil deeds to Jacob, their father. So, when the famine came on all the land and Joseph's brothers came to Egypt to buy food, he in turn says

> "You are spies! You have come to see the nakedness of the land" (Genesis 42:7-13).

They denied this by revealing their family history to Joseph (who remained incognito to them).

However, they are reminded of their guilty deed, when they told Joseph that they were originally twelve brothers. The youngest Benjamin was not with them and "one (Joseph) is no more."

In order to test them, one of them is sent back to fetch Benjamin and the remaining ten are cast into prison for three days, just as they had cast Joseph into a pit. They are thus faced with the same loss of liberty to which they had consigned Joseph. They had time to brood over their former treatment of Joseph and repent (Genesis 42:21-22).

Joseph now leads them another step forward. They are released from prison, except Simeon, who remains bound in prison as a surety for their return to Joseph with Benjamin. When they return with him, wanting to buy food, they are bidden to a feast with Joseph. Their seats are allotted to them according to their seniority, but to their amazement Benjamin, the youngest of the brothers, receives a larger portion of food than the rest.

They had envied Joseph in days gone by because their father Jacob had shown him preference over his other sons. Now the test is whether they harbour the same ill feelings toward Benjamin who had taken the place of Joseph in his father Jacob's affection. No ill feeling is shown by them at all and the feast was one of joy and gladness (Genesis 43:32-34).

There remained one final test which Joseph now submits his brothers to. Are they willing to suffer for their father's now favourite son Benjamin? To prove them on this point Joseph's drinking cup was concealed in Benjamin's sack by Joseph's steward, on his instructions.

When they were intercepted on their journey home by Joseph's steward, they submit themselves to a search, knowing that they were innocent of theft. But the cup is found in Benjamin's sack.

"Why have you repaid evil for good?"

was Joseph's question (Genesis 44:4). And now in fear and trembling, Judah and his brothers fall down to the ground before Joseph, thus fulfilling in all unconsciousness their brother Joseph's prophecy long ago in his dreams of the bowing sheaves and the obeisance of the sun, moon and stars (Genesis 42:6; 43:26; 44:14).

It is here that Judah intervenes with passionate pleadings for Benjamin. What a different Judah from the man who had previously said, regarding Joseph.

"Come and let us sell him to the Ishmaelites" (Genesis 37:27).

Let us read some of his most moving words in Genesis 44:30-34.

"Now therefore, when I come to your servant my father, and the boy is not with us, since his life is bound up in the boy's life, it will happen, when he sees that the boy is not with us, that he will die. So your servants will bring down the gray hair of your servant our father with sorrow to the grave. For your servant became surety for the boy to my father, saying, 'If I do not bring him back to you, then I shall bear the blame before my father for ever.' Now therefore, please let your servant remain instead of the boy as a slave to my lord, and let the boy go up with his brothers. For how shall I go up to my father if the boy is not with me, lest perhaps I see the evil that would come upon my father?"

Judah's simple compassionate plea proved the genuineness of their repentance and willingness to make amends. Joseph had at last brought his brother to humble confession and acknowledgement of their guilt. He ordered all outsiders out of the room and could not refrain himself from weeping aloud. (Genesis 45:1-8).

What a wonderful illustration here we have of God bringing good out of evil!

This does not excuse Joseph's brother from their evil act but it reveals the sovereignty of God in turning it to a good purpose. For:

"He works all things according to the counsel of His will" (Ephesians 1:11).

"For of Him and through Him are all things, to Whom be glory for the ages. Amen!" (Romans 11:36).

Joseph the man

What a marvellous man is Joseph! He who had innocently suffered at the hands of his brothers, without any bitterness or thought of revenge, disciplined them.

Step by step he led them to acknowledge their guilt and brought them to repentance. They had peace and harmony with him! He dealt with them on the basis of truth, yet showed them mercy. He caused them to face their transgression and realise their terrible guilt, and then showed them grace and forgiveness.

We have here, of course, a wonderful type of how God will lead Israel to repentance before their eyes are opened to recognise Jesus for whom he is.

There is much more of Joseph's life to comment on, but I will just content myself with a few more salient points:-

1. Moral courage

Joseph did not shrink form telling his father of his brothers' misdeeds, though they hated him and threatened to kill him. He refused to give in to Potiphar's wife, even though his life was in her hands for good or ill. He did not hesitate to tell the Chief Baker, the interpretation of his dream – his impending execution – even though it must have been a disagreeable task.

Do we declare "the whole counsel of God" to unbelievers? There is a tendency to be so enamoured with the Love and Grace of God, that we neglect to remind unbelievers that …

> "the wrath of God is revealed from heaven against all ungodliness (irreverence) and unrighteousness of men, who suppress the truth (of God) in unrighteousness" (Romans 1:18).

This is true both of the moral outcast and also the respectable "religious person" who seeks false security in church attendance and good works which are not motivated by the Holy Spirit and love to God! God makes no distinction:

> "for all have sinned and fall short of the glory of God." (Romans 3:23).

Have we the courage to tell forth this truth, which is so distasteful to unbelievers and invites persecution and suffering for Christ's sake?

2. Absolute trust in God's word

Believing God's Word, Joseph discovered God's hand in adversity and though his heart was wrung with anguish by the treatment of his brothers to him, yet he was able to pardon them, saying:

> "You meant it for evil against me, but God meant it for good" (Genesis 50:20).

Like Paul, he believed "that God works all things together for good to them that love him" (Romans 8:28), and this enabled him not to over-estimate his prison hardships, nor, when the Lord exalted him to be Prime Minister of Egypt, did he over estimate its honour and let it turn his head. The prison fetters did not sour his heart and the royal robe did not cause pride to raise its ugly head. The sense of God's presence kept him from despondency in affliction and from pride in prosperity. What a lesson for us!

3. Condescension to others

It is recorded that when Pharaoh sent for Joseph "he shaved himself and changed his raiment." Why were these words recorded? True he was ushered into the presence of the King of Egypt and he would be required to show proper respect by his appearance, but I think that Joseph was also willing in external matters to conform to the ways of the society in which he lived. He did not cause friction by refusing to conform to the traditional customs of the nation of Egypt in which he lived. Non-conformity to the age in which we live applies to its sinful practices, not its lawful customs. We should:

"render therefore to all their due: taxes to whom taxes are due; custom to whom custom; fear to whom fear; honour to whom honour" (Romans 13:7).

4. Magnanimity of spirit

The spirit of Joseph was surpassed only by that of our Lord and was the result of his faith in the universality of God's providence. His experience demonstrated that through all the evil that men intended to do to him, God prepared a more exceeding weight of glory. This expanded his capacity for sympathy and compassion towards others.

Joseph was dignified in his sufferings for righteousness. Abraham, Isaac and Jacob were victors of faith. They were noted for their mighty triumphs. They appeal to the heroic in us. They demonstrated the active virtues. Their lives illustrate that "nothing is impossible with God."

Joseph was not only a victor of faith but also a victim of faith, and it takes a deeper obedience of faith to suffer for God than to accomplish something for Him. To be obedient and suffer are greater than to do! For it has been graciously granted you, for Christ sake:

"not only to believe in him, but also to suffer for his sake" (Philippians 1:29).

A dispensational application

There is a dispensational side to Joseph's treatment of his brothers. Is it not a type of the gracious way Christ Himself is dealing with His chosen nation Israel? The rejection and crucifixion of our Lord by that nation, was portrayed in type by the casting of Joseph by his brothers into a pit. His subsequent exaltation to Prime Minister of Egypt portrays the resurrection and exaltation of our Lord to the right hand of God (the place of favour).

The disciplinary treatment of his brothers by Joseph, depicts the disciplining of Israel by God. The destruction of Jerusalem by Titus in AD 70 and the massacre of the Jews; the scattering of those who escaped among the nations; their intermittent persecution and finally the Great Tribulation, yet future, are all judgments by the hand of God to bring Israel to repentance and restoration. Just as Joseph made himself known to his brothers, so shall our Lord be manifest to Israel at His Second Coming. "They will look on Him Whom they pierced" and mourn their evil deed to Him. Yet God has used that evil deed to bring blessing to Israel in the future, when they are restored and fulfil the purpose God has chosen them for – to bring spiritual and material blessing, under their Messiah Christ as Lord, to the whole world.

The blood of Christ's cross has brought blessing and salvation to us, members of Christ's Body, whose future destiny is in the heavenly realms (Ephesians 1:3; 2:6,7; 3:10; Philippians 3:20; Colossians 3:1-4). By that same precious blood, God's great purpose of the ages will be completed, by the reconciliation and heading up of all in the heavens and on earth (Ephesians 1:10; 1 Corinthians 15:28; Colossians 1:20; Philippians 2:9-11).

Joseph's death

Joseph's career concluded, as it began, with an expression of unbounded faith in the Word of God, looking forward to the resurrection when he will take his place with the redeemed of Israel in the Promised Land (Genesis 50:24-25).

Conclusion

May the Holy Spirit of God apply the relevant lesson from the life of Joseph to our minds and hearts; to our spiritual benefit through faith obedience to God's will in our lives in our day and age!

More on Joseph

Portraits of the Patriarchs

By William Henry, Andrew Marple, Michael Penny and Sylvia Penny

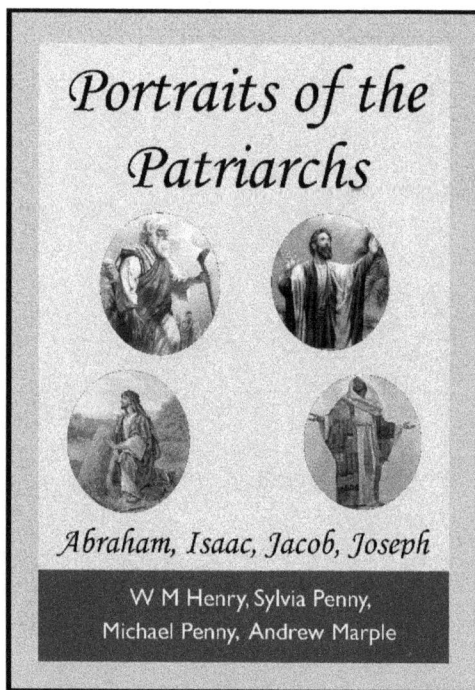

Portraits of the Patriarchs is based on Abraham, Isaac, Jacob and Joseph.

The four authors do an excellent job of not only bringing before us the important issues in the lives of the four patriarchs (i.e. lessons in history).

However, they also, in considering the lives and experiences of Abraham, Isaac, Jacob and Joseph, draw out lessons of faith and practice which are applicable to 21st century Christians.

****

Further details of this book can be seen on
www.obt.org.uk

It can be ordered from the website
and also from

The Open Bible Trust,
Fordland Mount, Upper Basildon,
Reading, RG8 8LU, UK.

It also available as an eBook
from Amazon and Apple,
and also as a KDP paperback from Amazon.

Free sample

For a free sample of
the Open Bible Trust's magazine *Search*,
please email

admin@obt.org.uk

or visit

www.obt.org.uk/search

About the author

James Poole was born in Finchley, London, in 1909 and took a course in Business Training at the City of London College. During his working years he was employed by various institutions and banks in the City of London. When he wrote this booklet he was enjoying retirement with his wife in Eastbourne, Sussex, but has since fallen asleep in Christ.

Also by James Poole

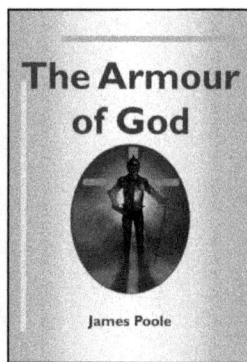

Abraham

James Poole

Isaac

James Poole

Jacob

James Poole

Joseph

James Poole

Notes on Ephesians

James Poole

The Armour of God

James Poole

Practical Christianity — James Poole — THE OPEN BIBLE TRUST

The Seven Stages of A Believer's Exaltation In Christ — James Poole

Notes on Ephesians — James Poole

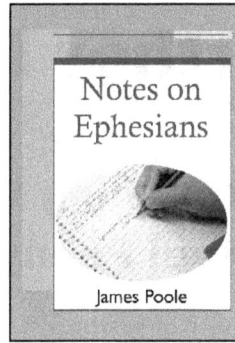

Further details of all the books here can be seen
on **www.obt.org.uk**

The can be ordered from the website
and also from

The Open Bible Trust,
Fordland Mount, Upper Basildon,
Reading, RG8 8LU, UK.

They are also available as eBooks
from Amazon and Apple,
and also as KDP paperbacks from Amazon.

Further Reading

Approaching the Bible
Michael Penny

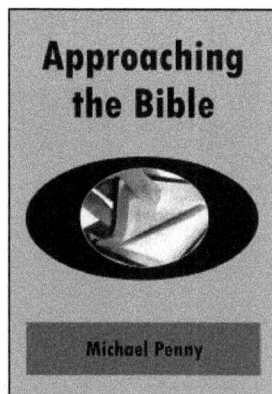

In easy to understand steps, and with many interesting examples, Michael Penny provides the rational for the view that before we try to *apply* any passage in the Bible to ourselves, we should discover first what it meant to those to whom its words were initially addressed. The book advocates that this is best done by considering the passage under the following headings:

1) **Who** said or wrote it;
2) to **Whom** was it said or written, or concerning **Whom** was it said or written;
3) **Where** it was said or written, or concerning **Where** was it said or written;
4) **What** was said or written;
5) **When** was it said or written, or concerning **When** was it said or written;
6) **Why** was it said or written.

Applying these six **"W"** rules puts the passage into its proper context and gives us the right perspective on it. Only after doing this can we determine:

7) **W**hether the passage applies to our situation and what the correct application is.

It is the *consistent* use of these **Seven Ws** which helps us discover the right and relevant application of any passage to our lives.

****

This book, and the one on the next page, can be ordered from **www.obt.org.uk** and from

The Open Bible Trust,
Fordland Mount, Upper Basildon,
Reading, RG8 8LU, UK.

40 Problem Passages
Michael Penny

This book is a sequel to *Approaching the Bible*.

The 7 Ws advocated in *Approaching the Bible* are applied to 40 difficult to understand passages. There are, of course, far more than 40 Problem Passages in the Bible. However, in this book Michael Penny not only solves these *40 Problem Passages*, but in doing so he equips the reader with a method by which many, many more hard to understand and difficult passages can be understood and successfully applied to the life of the believer today.

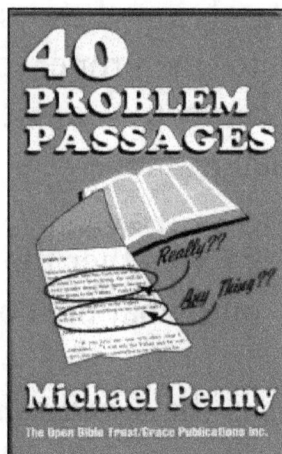

****

This book, and the ones on the previous pages,
are also available as eBooks
from Amazon and Apple,

and also as KDP paperbacks from Amazon.

About this book

Joseph

In this publication, the life and person of Joseph is considered concisely yet comprehensively. In Joseph we have a believer who is an example to us all of how to persevere when the going gets tough.

He is also seen to be a type of Christ and we have two sections in which the author draws many helpful parallels between Joseph and Jesus.

Publications of The Open Bible Trust must be in accordance with its evangelical, fundamental and dispensational basis. However, beyond this minimum, writers are free to express whatever beliefs they may have as their own understanding, provided that the aim in so doing is to further the object of The Open Bible Trust. A copy of the doctrinal basis is available at

www.obt.org.uk/doctrinal-basis

or from:

THE OPEN BIBLE TRUST
Fordland Mount, Upper Basildon,
Reading, RG8 8LU, GB

www.ingramcontent.com/pod-product-compliance
Lightning Source LLC
Chambersburg PA
CBHW060609030426
42337CB00018B/3013